Thoughts & Prayers for the Post-Partum Mom

E. Danielle Butler

Unless otherwise noted, Scriptures are taken from HOLY BIBLE, NEW INTERNATIONAL VERSION. Copyright 1973, 1978, 1984 by International Bible Society. Used by permission of Zondervan Publishing House.

Scripture quotations marked "ESV" are taken from The Holy Bible: English Standard Version, Copyright 2001, Wheaton: Good News Publishers. Used by permission. All rights reserved.

Scripture quotations marked "NASB" are taken from the New American Standard Bible, Copyright ©1960, 1962, 1963, 1968, 1971, 1972, 1973, 1975, 1977, 1995 by The Lockman Foundation, La Habra, CA. All rights reserved. Used by Permission.

Scriptures marked KJV are taken from the KING JAMES VERSION (KJV): KING JAMES VERSION, public domain.

Scripture quotations marked MSG are taken from THE MESSAGE, copyright © 1993, 1994, 1995, 1996, 2000, 2001, 2002 by Eugene H. Peterson. Used by permission of NavPress. All rights reserved.

Thoughts & Prayers for the Postpartum Mom

EvyDani Books, LLC

evydanibooks@gmail.com

Copyright © 2017 by E. Danielle Butler

All Rights Reserved. No part of this publication may be reproduced, distributed, or transmitted in any form or by any means, including photocopying, recording, or other electronic or mechanical methods, without the prior written permission of the publisher.

ISBN: 978-1-7361534-4-4 (paperback); 978-1-7361534-3-7 (ebook)

Printed in the United States of America

This is dedicated to all the magnificent moms who support me on my own journey in Mommyhood.

THANK YOU

I would like to thank my husband, Brandon, for choosing me to join the parenting journey with him. I love you babe!

Also, thank you to Zoe & Zachary for helping me be the best version of myself. Love you guys!

Introduction

Great job Mom! You did it! You birthed a beautiful baby. At times the journey seemed long and arduous. Other times you were overjoyed with anticipation. Now you're settling into your new life. Even if you've done this many times before, each time is different and each child unique- your life is changing AGAIN. There are sure to be some sleepless nights ahead, some exhausted giggles and seemingly a million memories to be made in such a short time span. There may be many people checking in on baby. But I'm here to check on you. My thoughts and prayers are focused on your well-being. My words exist to encourage you, to support you and perhaps even sustain you. As I write this, I am six months postpartum with my second baby. So really, I am right here with you. I'm daily reminding myself that this is a journey. I'm working to be kind towards myself - to be gentle and understanding - to be mindful, to be gracious and most importantly to be loving towards myself. And it's hard. Some days it seems selfish and downright impossible. But... it's necessary. And just as it is necessary for me, it is necessary for you. It is important for you to take care of you. As you go through this process of healing and changing, adding to your roles and responsibilities, know that someone is praying for you. Someone is thinking of you. Feel free to write in this book. In fact, I highly recommend the cathartic release that occurs through the process of journaling. Chronicle your experience as you adjust to your new normal. Note how you feel and what you're experiencing. Be honest about the things that went well and forgiving of those that didn't. Don't be afraid to make this book all about you. And no, it's not selfish; it's essential.

Be Refreshed!

Danielle

Gracious Father God,
I thank you for the beautiful vessel holding this book. I thank you for your faithfulness towards her in blessing her with children. Lord, my desire is for her to know your love in this season of transition. Allow your Holy Spirit to be her comforter and guide. May your grace and favor be evident to her as she cares for her new little one. Help her to recognize that you care for her all the more. Father, draw her closer to you. Let your strength be perfected in her weakness. In Jesus' name I pray. Amen.

> **2 Cor 12:9 (ESV)**
> But he said to me, "My grace is sufficient for you, for my power is made perfect in weakness." Therefore I will boast all the more gladly of my weaknesses, so that the power of Christ may rest upon me.

Permission to Reflect

Wherever you are on your postpartum journey, reflection is always warranted. Take the time to identify where you are, how far you've come and where you'd like to go. Reflection provides an opportunity for you to check in with self and maintain a more balanced sense of well-being. Reflection allows you space to admit flaws and mistakes and to rejoice in the good things. Keep a journal to record your trek. Make the habit of emptying your thoughts and feelings. Your thoughts and feelings matter. They are important. They are significant. Give them their due space. Schedule reflection time at regular intervals. Note any patterns; replicate the good ones and eliminate the unproductive ones.

REFLECT: WHEN WAS THE LAST TIME YOU WERE ALONE WITH YOUR TRUE THOUGHTS AND FEELINGS?

Dear Heavenly Father,
   Thank you for bringing us on this journey called life. Search our

hearts. Help us to give ourselves permission to reflect in truth. Grant us courage to face all that we are responsible for in this season. In Jesus' name. Amen.

Galatians 6:4
Each one should test their own actions. Then they can take pride in themselves alone, without comparing themselves to someone else

Give It Time

Don't rush. Don't rush this moment, this process, this transition. Don't rush it. Whether it's giving your body time to heal or anxiously awaiting baby to sleep through the night. Even if it's getting back on your feet to do all of the driving, cooking and cleaning – don't rush. Whatever your "it" is – give it time. Allow your mind time to process. Give your body time to reset. Grant your emotions permission to run their course.

REFLECT: WHAT "IT" ARE YOU RUSHING TODAY?

Dear Lord,

Thank you for this moment. Help us to appreciate this moment which we will never see again. Allow us to bask in the beauty or lesson that it provides. Father grant us peace to transition and wisdom to pace ourselves on the journey. We are grateful for the experience Lord. In Jesus' name. Amen.

Jeremiah 2:25 (MSG)

"Slow down. Take a deep breath. What's the hurry? Why wear yourself out? Just what are you after anyway? But you say, 'I can't help it. I'm addicted to alien gods. I can't quit.'

BE KIND

Be kind to yourself today. Forget the mistakes and things that didn't go as planned. Forgive yourself for the choices and actions that didn't work out as you intended. Instead, focus on the things that you have done well. Accept your imperfections and praise your progress. Be kind to yourself today.

REFLECT: WHAT HAVE YOU DONE WELL IN THE LAST 24-48 HOURS?

Heavenly Father,
    Teach us to be kind to ourselves. Let the same gracious nature that You have be added unto us. Allow the kindness that we distribute to others to be reflected within. Elevate our acceptance of self as flawed, yet worthy. We thank you Lord for the fruit of kindness being evident in our lives. In Jesus' name, amen.

Mark 12:31 (ESV)

The second is this: 'You shall love your neighbor as yourself.' There is no other commandment greater than these."

Be Grateful

With so many changes happening at once, it can be easy to overlook the small blessings happening right in front of you. Take a moment and look around where you are. Take note of the things that you are grateful for. You are not where you started and certainly not where you will end up. Even if things are not all that you would like for them to be in this moment, be grateful knowing that it could be worse. When you think on the good things, there's no room in your mind to think on the troublesome. Two thoughts can't simultaneously exist. Choose the thoughts of gratitude. They will bombard the negative ones.

REFLECT: WHAT ARE YOU GRATEFUL FOR RIGHT NOW?

Dear God,
   We enter into your gates with thanksgiving. Help us to recognize and celebrate the good things that are in our lives right now. God, we have life, health and strength; for that alone we are grateful. We thank you for an

opportunity to be mothers. We are grateful for provision, Lord. We choose the attitude of gratitude today. In Jesus' Name. Amen.

Ephesians 5:20
always giving thanks to God the Father for everything,
in the name of our Lord Jesus Christ

You are Not Alone

Some nights you may find yourself awake while the entire house rests. It can be an isolating and lonely feeling. In those sleepless nights, when the house is quiet – remember you are not alone. Accept the silence and take a few minutes to embrace yourself and receive the tranquility that has come to you. As you look at those sleeping under your watch, know that there is someone who is watching over and cares for you the same way. Exhale. Receive. When it feels like no one else understands – remember, you are not alone.

Reflect: What is your favorite thing to do when it's quiet around the house?

Heavenly Father,
  We acknowledge our feelings of loneliness and lay them at your feet. Lord, we know that you will never leave or nor forsake us. You'll also stick closer to us than any brother. Holy Spirit, help us remember these things on

the days when we feel so alone. Comfort us and allow us to rest in your presence. Refresh us in the times of silence and solitude. Fortify us for the next active moment. In Jesus' name. Amen.

Isaiah 41:10

So do not fear, for I am with you; do not be dismayed, for I am your God. I will strengthen you and help you; I will uphold you with my righteous right hand.

New Normal

Whether this is your first baby or your fourth, welcoming a new life into your home, family and life is a significant change. Adjusting can be a tremendous challenge. As you journey through these first few days, weeks and months, take note of the things that work for you and your family. Adjust your new normal to be a constant reflection of those things that work well. Eliminate those things that have become cumbersome or no longer make sense for your current life space. You have the power to define your new normal and not let it define you.

REFLECT: WHAT HAS BEEN THE BIGGEST CHANGE OR ADJUSTMENT TO YOUR LIFE SINCE YOUR NEW ARRIVAL?

Lord God,

We are in a season of great transition. Show us how to walk in this new place of expansion. Illuminate the best ways for us to guide and support our family. Give us discernment, O' Lord. We thank you for the wisdom to apply what works and the strength to reject those things that are not for us in this season. We pursue your peace in every area of our lives. In Christ Jesus' name, we pray. Amen.

Ecclesiastes 3:1 (ESV)
For everything there is a season, and a time for every matter under heaven

Feel the Feeling

Having a baby produces a lot of emotions that go much deeper than just hormones. There's fear, joy, excitement, anticipation. Nervousness, sadness, shock and love are also often present. And the wild thing is you can experience more than one on totally different ends of the spectrum at a time. But here's the important thing to note: it is acceptable for you to feel all of those feelings. It is okay for you to experience an emotion that you haven't had before or be exposed to one at a deeper level than ever before. Feel those feelings. Know that these moments that are happening won't be relived, at least not in the same way. Feel those feelings. Acknowledge them. Take note of what occurrence invoked the feeling. And if you find yourself stuck in the valley of overwhelm or negative emotion, don't be afraid to ask for help.

REFLECT: WHICH EMOTIONS HAVE BEEN THE MOST PRESENT OVER THE LAST WEEK?

Dear Lord,

We are feeling so many things right now. Help us to appropriately process the feelings of being a new mom. Lord lead us to peace and stability in our emotions. Nudge us when we are out of balance emotionally, that we may be on track. Give us the discernment to recognize the presence of hopelessness, depression and sadness; grant us the courage to reach out for help. Surround us with people who have our best interest at heart. Lord, we accept your countenance of joy and peace as our portion. In Jesus' name, amen.

Ecclesiastes 3:4 (ESV)
A time to weep, and a time to laugh; a time to mourn,
    and a time to dance;

Overwhelm

Everything is happening so fast! The days may even seem to run together. It is easy to get overwhelmed. It can become easy to say that you should be able to do something on your own or to take on too much. But that is not your portion or position in this season. It is more important that you set boundaries, for yourself and others, to ensure that you aren't constantly trudging in the place of overwhelm. Ask for help. It's not a sign of weakness, but rather the mark of strength, value and accountability.

REFLECT: IN WHAT AREA(S) ARE YOU FEELING OVERWHELMED RIGHT NOW?

Dear God,
 Sometimes all that is happening feels like too much. Father, we give it over to you. When our minds are racing and our hearts are heavy, we pause to experience your love and peace. Lord lead us in confidence to the

abundant life you have promised us. We do not cave under being overwhelmed, instead we yield. We yield to abundant peace, abundant order, abundant strength and abundant confidence. It's in Jesus Christ's name we pray, amen.

Psalm 63:1 (KJV)
From the end of the earth will I cry unto thee, when my heart is overwhelmed: lead me to the rock that is higher than I

Doing Too Much

You may have heard the saying that someone is "doing too much" and as a new mom this may accurately describe you. Perhaps you are nursing the baby and trying to do laundry and reply to people's messages on social media. Maybe you are trying to juggle dinner, complete homework with an older child and clean the house before Dad gets home. With a new baby, you may just be doing too much. It is okay if the floors aren't spotless. Yes, I see that pile of unfolded laundry over there too, at least it's is clean. Sustaining life, yours and baby's, is hard. Try to avoid overdoing it wherever you can. Accept help. Delegate.

Reflect: Are you doing too much? What things can you do to help alleviate some of the strain?

Gracious Father,

Thank you for this time in our lives of experiencing new birth. We come today acknowledging that we may be doing too much. Lord, even you took time over the creation of the earth. You didn't do it all at once, took a rest day and still got it all done. Help us to break our tasks and responsibilities into realistic pieces for this time in our lives. Illuminate a path for us to avoid doing too much. In Your son's name. Amen.

Exodus 18:18
You and these people who come to you will only wear yourselves out. The work is too heavy for you; you cannot handle it alone

You are Capable

If you're honest, there are probably some days when you wonder if you are capable of handling all of this new found responsibility. You may even wonder if you are capable of experiencing anything that resembles normalcy. Be encouraged – you are capable. You are capable of achieving adequate self-care. You are capable of pouring out love to your little one and others around you. You are capable of living a fulfilling life. You are capable. YOU ARE CAPABLE.

Reflect: Is there something that you recently felt incapable of doing? What adjustments can you make that would allow you to be reminded of your capabilities in that area?

Dear Lord,
    Help us to see that we are capable. In our weakness and inadequacies, your strength makes us capable. Allow us to maintain our sense of worth,

value, contribution and capability. Father, we know that we are created in your image. When we fall short of that, remind us that we are capable in you. In Jesus' name, amen.

> **2 Corinthians 3:5 (NASB)**
> Not that we are adequate in ourselves to consider anything as coming from ourselves, but our adequacy is from God

Sleepless Nights

No doubt there will be some nights where sleep is impossible: from gas to teething to light sleeping and everything in between. Remind yourself that it won't be like this always. The current circumstances and conditions are temporary. Rest when you can. Embrace the sunlight often. And on those nights when sleep seems so far away, find a source of laughter until you can recharge. Be encouraged – sleep will come.

REFLECT: Have you established a sleep routine yet? How is it working?

Gracious Lord,
   Grant your daughter the grace she needs to endure the sleepless nights attached to this season of her life. Your Word reminds us that everything has a season, and we know that this is just a season. Give her times of refreshing Lord and show her how to adjust her perspective. Help her to identify the best ways to get her rest in the midst of it all Father. Allow her

village to rise up and provide assistance where they can. I thank you Lord that she will not grow weary in the well-doing of caring for her children. I thank you Lord that she rests under the shadow of your wing. And Lord if she is up for reasons of worry and anxiety, I thank you for bringing peace to her mind. I thank you that your Word tells us that you give sleep to those who you love. So Lord we know that you will give her sleep according your word. In Jesus' name, amen.

Psalm 4:8
In peace I will lie down and sleep, for you alone, Lord,
    make me dwell in safety

WORRY

Society and the internet make extreme worrying possible. We have a toe ache, Google it and BAM – we're convinced we only have three days to live based on some extreme, overly detailed warning. It's the same way with having children. Yes, there are things that we are and should be concerned about. But we don't have to worry. Use wisdom, but don't worry.

REFLECT: WHAT THINGS HAVE YOU BEEN WORRIED ABOUT LATELY?

Dear Lord,

Right now, we choose to cast our worry in your direction. We know you to be a keeper, a provider, a protector and a sustainer. Help us to rest in knowing that you've got us covered in every area of life. Help us to use wisdom and consult you instead of wallowing in worry. Let us see you as our source and answer concerning all things. In Jesus' mighty name, amen.

Psalm 55:22
Cast your cares on the Lord and he will sustain you; he will never let the righteous be shaken

Rejecting Guilt

As a mom, it is easy to feel guilty about so many things. Choose to reject mom guilt and put off any shame. Do not feel guilty about taking time to recover. Avoid blame that would tell you that you are not doing enough, when in fact you are doing your very best. Turn away from thoughts that would have you believe that you have done something wrong in caring for yourself. If you have made a mistake, forgive yourself. Resist the temptation to let guilt settle in.

REFLECT: IS THERE SOMETHING THAT YOU HAVE BEEN FEELING GUILTY ABOUT? IS IT SOMETHING THAT YOU CAN CHANGE?

Father,
 Today we choose forgiveness, not just for others, but for ourselves. We come against the feelings of guilt for not doing, being, feeling, acting a certain way in this season. The world would have us to believe that we are

not doing enough. We choose to operate in your wisdom and release ourselves from the bondage of unmet unrealistic expectations. In Jesus' name, amen.

Romans 8:1 (ESV)

There is therefore now no condemnation for those who are in Christ Jesus.

AGAINST RESENTMENT

Have you noticed how quickly and easily resentment and bitterness can creep in? Sometimes it starts as something minor and then you focus on it or think back to it, and it grows. Next thing you know you're resenting your partner because a baby is not hanging from their chest in the middle of the night. Or you're resenting a friend because she still has time to go get her hair and nails done without booking a sitter. Regardless of the infraction, it is important that you don't allow resentment and bitterness to take root in you. Remember that the circumstances are temporary.

REFLECT: IS THERE SOMEONE OR SOMETHING TOWARD WHICH YOU'VE FELT A DEEPENING SENSE OF RESENTMENT? WHAT IS CAUSING THE RESENTMENT? (I.E. WHAT DO YOU FEEL YOU ARE MISSING, NOT RECEIVING OR ACHIEVING?

Dear Lord,

Help us to guard our hearts against resentment and bitterness. Show us how to embrace the season that we are in with gratitude and not be jealous of the others that we are observing. Help us not to allow our relationships to deteriorate because of resentment. In Jesus' name. Amen.

Ephesians 4:31
Get rid of all bitterness, rage and anger, brawling and slander, along with every form of malice.

More Than a Mom

These days it feels like your gifts and talents rest in providing milk, changing diapers and rocking irritability to peace. Yes, you are a mother. But you are so much more than that. You are a woman. It is okay for you to relate to yourself in other spaces. It is advisable that you take time to be you without all of the other roles attached you. Stand tall in the skin you're in, even if only for a few minutes per day.

Reflect: Who are you when you're not in mom mode?

Lord God,
You have created us to be fruitful and multiply. Help us to see that it's not just in our ability to produce children, but in other areas of life too. Show us the other areas of our lives where we are bearing fruit – work, relationship, community and many other areas. Remind us that our purpose is greater than motherhood. We are called and ordained by you to

be so much more. Allow us to see ourselves as you see us, in all of our multifaceted splendor, in your likeness. In Christ's name. Amen.

Ephesians 2:10
For we are God's handiwork, created in Christ Jesus to do good works, which God prepared in advance for us to do

In Your Eyes

In your eyes, there's so much truth. They share whether you are tired or hurt. They indicate when you are surprised or full of joy. Your little one is undoubtedly spending hours staring into them. They are searching for love, guidance, acceptance, reassurance and so much more. As they gaze deep into the eyes that are the most familiar, they find comfort, confidence and strength. Take a look and you will see all of the things that make you all that you are. Look beyond the telling bags and weary gaze. As you look, it is my hope that you see strength. I pray that you see hope and promise. I believe that you will see resilience and persistence. I trust that you will acknowledge your journey and all the amazing things that it has brought thus far.

REFLECT: WHAT DO YOU SEE WHEN YOU LOOK INTO YOUR EYES IN THE MIRROR?

Dear Lord,

Illuminate our eyes with your joy and light. Add laughter that our eyes may reflect happiness. Father, if we see worn eyes, show us ways to rest. If we see discouragement, encourage us. Show us peace and confidence in our eyes. Let us see ourselves as you see us, fearfully and wonderfully made. In Jesus' name, amen.

Matthew 6:22
The eye is the lamp of the body. If your eyes are healthy, your whole body will be full of light.

Beauty is in the Eye of the Beholder

Many times, giving birth allows you to see yourself through another lens. You have this beautiful being whose exquisiteness is unmatched by any other source you've encountered. And then it hits you, they've got your eyes, or nose, or smile, or eyebrows, or expression – or some combination of them all. But you may not be ready to acknowledge the fact that those elements of beauty can be traced back to the greatest source of beauty – YOU. Today I want you to embrace your beauty. Even if you have never felt it before, today, you are beautiful, even more than the day before. If you need a little reassurance, look into the face of the little one. Remember how beautiful those features are? Yes, that's you reflected, and you are just that beautiful too.

Reflect: What is your most beautiful physical feature?

Father God,

We know that you created us beautifully, in your likeness. Increase our self-esteem. Enhance our perception of our physical selves. Highlight the beauty that you see that we should see. Remind us Father that you made no mistakes in creating us. Help us to pass on our acceptance and confidence of beauty to our children. In Your son Jesus' name, we pray. Amen.

> **Psalm 139:14**
>
> I praise you because I am fearfully and wonderfully made; your works are wonderful, I know that full well.

Your Body is Beautiful

Your body is an amazing vessel. It has carried life. It has stretched. It has sacrificed. It has provided all things to another. Your body is incredible. Although it may not look or feel like it (to you) right now, it is beautiful. Every mark, out of place area and seemingly different than before section is a reminder. It is a reminder of the great feat you just partook of. Each soft spot, every sag and the individual marks of skin once stretched serve as a recap of the wonderful journey you have just completed. Whether you are on day one or month 10, your body is beautiful.

Reflect: What is the biggest physical change you have struggled with since having baby? What can the change be a positive reminder of?

Dear Lord,
   Thank you for creating our bodies and allowing us to produce. Father,

help us to see our bodies as beautiful creations crafted by you. Give us the confidence to walk boldly in the stunning skin and frames we are in. In Christ Jesus' name, amen.

Song of Solomon 4:7
You are altogether beautiful, my darling; there is no flaw in you

Naked & Unashamed

What do you see when you look in the mirror? Better yet, have you taken the time to really look in the mirror? Not just at your face and hair, but at your entire body? Yes, it has probably changed. But I hope you see the beauty in it too. I hope that you recognize the strength and resilience that it represents. Will you acknowledge its capability to sustain life and produce greatness? Will you accept your naked body and all of the truth it tells, the journey it represents? I encourage you to take time and stand before your mirror, yourself and your maker naked and unashamed.

REFLECT: WHAT ARE THE GOOD THINGS THAT YOU NOTICE ABOUT YOUR BODY WHEN YOU ARE NAKED?

Father God,
  Forgive us for not seeing ourselves in the beauty and likeness of you. Help us return to a place of comfort with our naked bodies, that we may be

unashamed. Help us to change our perspectives; allow us to accept our bodies. We are fearfully and wonderfully made. In Jesus' matchless name, amen.

Genesis 2:25 (ESV)
And the man and his wife were both naked and were not ashamed

Resuming Intimacy

Depending on where you are in your postpartum journey, physical intimacy may be the absolute last thing on your mind. But eventually the time will come for you to reconnect. Recognize that adjustments may be required. Be open. Be open to change. Be willing. Be patient. Be forgiving. But most of all be honest. Be honest in what works best. Be honest about how you feel. You might not feel sexy right away. That's okay. Or you may be a mountain lion on the prowl. That's okay too. Remember he knows that you've had a baby. He's watched your body do its thing over the last few months, so he expects that something might be different. Rest assured that eventually things will be back on track. And there's always the possibility that it continues to get even better.

REFLECT: HOW DO YOU FEEL RIGHT NOW ABOUT INTIMACY?

Dear Lord,

As we are in transition, help us to remain in physical, mental and spiritual intimacy with our partner. Allow us to grow deeper in our relationships with them. Restore passion if it has become absent. Turn our desires to one another for continued connection and renewal. In Jesus' name, amen.

Song of Solomon 1:2
Let him kiss me with the kisses of his mouth—for your love is more delightful than wine.

Friendships

You've had the baby and now there seems to be a strain on some of your friendships. You are missing activities, don't get to chat as much as you used to (if at all), and social media is reminding you that the world continues to move on even though you feel stuck in mommy mode. Yes, your friendships will undergo some change. But it is important that you remain connected with others rather than retreating into isolation. As you define your new normal, opportunities will arise for you to readjust your relationships and still connect with others in a way that is meaningful. Friendship is necessary.

REFLECT: WHICH OF YOUR FRIENDSHIPS HAVE BEEN IMPACTED THE MOST SINCE HAVING YOUR BABY? WHAT CAN YOU DO TO RECONNECT?

Lord God,
   Thank you for true, strong, loyal friendships. Help us to maintain

those relationships, even in the face of change. Allow us to continue to connect with our friends. Teach us to readjust as necessary so that we are still getting the support and love that we need from our relationships. In your son's name, amen.

Proverbs 17:17
A friend loves at all times, and a brother is born for adversity.

You Time

As the mom of a little one, sometimes finding time for self can seem impossible. But you've done a great job of grabbing a few snatches here and there to read this book. Go forward in your journey as a mom remembering that, next to God, you are your most valuable resource. If you are not renewed and refreshed, it becomes increasingly difficult to sustain the other things you are responsible for. Establish a lifestyle of self-care. You need it. You deserve it. You are worth it.

REFLECT: WHAT IS YOUR SELF-CARE ROUTINE?

Father God,

Thank you for our lives, health and strength. We thank you for reminding us that we are important and good in your sight. Help us to value ourselves enough to take care of our temples internally and externally. Show us when and how to take time to be the best versions of ourselves. In Jesus' wonderful name, amen.

. . .

Proverbs 11:17 (ESV)
A man who is kind benefits himself, but a cruel man hurts himself.

In Closing

Dear Friend,

    I am so glad that you joined me on this journey. Being a new mom is certainly not easy. I like to describe it as one of the greatest challenges yet most amazing rewards of my entire life. Thank you for allowing me to pray with you. Thank you for allowing me to speak good things and gentle reminders to you. The time you have spent and thoughts that you have shared in this space are sacred. They represent your truth and commitment to self. That's amazing! It took me forever to find and honor that space in my life with my first child. As you continue your journey, it is my sincerest hope that you remember that you are just as important as the little one in your world. I pray that you recognize, accept and celebrate all of the things that make you wonderful. Remember, it's not easy, but it's so worth it. Not only that, you can do it!

With Appreciation for You & Confidence in Your Journey,

Danielle

Quick Reference Scriptures

Anxiety
- Psalm 94:19
- Philippians 4:6-9
- Matthew 6:25-3
- John 14:27
- 1 Peter 5:7-9

Rest
- Genesis 2:3
- Exodus 18:18
- Psalm 127:2
- Matthew 11:28
- Hebrews 4:9-11

Self-Care & Identity
- Jeremiah 29:11
- 3 John 1:2

Ephesians 2:10
Ephesians 5:29
Philippians 4:8

Support Resources

Should you find yourself in need of additional support during your postpartum journey, here are a few resources to keep at hand. Please keep in mind that you can also reach out to your primary care physician, OB/GYN and pediatrician for additional support.

Postpartum Support International
postpartum.net | 1-800-944-4773

Office on Women's Health
Womenshealth.gov | 1-800-994-9662

National Suicide Prevention Lifeline
988lifeline.org | 988

About the Author

E. Danielle Butler has an affinity for writing and the arts. She believes in the power of words and the magic of imagination. An acclaimed conversation catalyst, Danielle is recognized as an energetic thought provoker with a passion for sharing knowledge. Through writing and speaking, Danielle embraces a personal mission to produce content that provokes change and inspires action. Her first devotional, *Mood Swing: 21 Days to Peace, Joy and Freedom of Mind,* was released in 2014. In 2017, she released three children's books in *The Adventures of Zoe & Zachary* series.

Danielle is a certified personal development coach. With a Bachelor of Arts in Theater and Master of Management, she brings a unique perspective to all she approaches. Her professional background includes performing arts instruction, time as a classroom teacher, and nonprofit administration.

Danielle resides in Atlanta with her husband and two children. When she's not taking in the sights and sounds around the city, she can be found enjoying great food. Danielle is available for readings and speaking engagements. For contact and bookings, reach out at evydanibooks@gmail.com.

facebook.com/evydanib
twitter.com/evydanib
instagram.com/evydanib

Also by E. Danielle Butler

Mood Swing: 21 Days to Peace, Joy and Freedom of Mind

The Maple Crew: A Memoir by Jessie Maple

Homeschool How?! The Practical Guide to Homeschool and Digital Learning for Working Parents

Zoe's Bun – The Adventures of Zoe & Zachary

Zoe Gets a Brother – The Adventures of Zoe & Zachary

Zachary Goes to School – The Adventures of Zoe & Zachary

Adventures of the Mind Creative Writing Journal for the Young Imagination – The Adventures of Zoe & Zachary

www.ingramcontent.com/pod-product-compliance
Lightning Source LLC
Chambersburg PA
CBHW021124080526
44587CB00010B/631